The Escape

OF A BURNING HEART

GURNOOR K. CHADDA

Presentation by *BookLeaf Publishing*

Web: www.bookleafpub.com
E-mail: info@bookleafpub.com

ISBN: 9789363307018

First edition 2024

To my revered mentor,
Gurdial Singh Bedi

CONTENTS

ACKNOWLEDGEMENT

The universe has been benevolent towards me, for gracing me with the ability to put my feelings and thoughts in the chain of words through poetry. I am grateful beyond words to the almighty for such benevolence, and for bringing such events and triggers in my life, that inspired me to write. I believe poetry in this book is truly a reflection, of what universe wants to convey through me, rather than it being completely my own creation.

I am grateful to my mentor, my godfather, Gurdial Singh Bedi, for sowing a seed of success in my mind and heart. He has been a constant support and guide in all my highs and lows. Without him I was nothing and would have been nothing. I am thankful to him for believing in me, for making me believe in the greater power of universe and for bringing this book to life.

I am also grateful to my parents, my family and friends, for being the backbone in my journey, and for being readily available with suggestions and solutions whenever I needed them. Special thanks to my father who made it his task to give wings to my dreams be it financially or emotionally. Had it not been him, this book could never have reached the hands that are holding it now.

I would also like to extend my thanks to Book Leaf Publication, for bringing this book out to readers. My publishing journey with them has really been smooth.

ACKNOWLEDGMENT

[illegible] has [illegible] inspired me, for teaching [illegible] and [illegible] [illegible] [illegible] that [illegible] believe poetry in this book is truly inspired me to write, I believe poetry in this book is truly a reflection of what [illegible] wants to convey through [illegible] completely our own creation.

[illegible] and [illegible] support and guide [illegible] would have been [illegible] I am thankful to [illegible] believe in the greater [illegible] bringing this book to life.

I am also grateful to my parents, my family and friends for [illegible] in my journey, and for being [illegible] with suggestions and solutions when I needed them. Special thanks to my father who [illegible] to give wings to my dreams both financially and emotionally. Without him, this book could never have [illegible] holding now.

I would also like to extend my thanks to Book Leaf Publications for bringing this book out to readers. My publishing journey with them has really been smooth.

THE LIFE

I was figuring, who I'm?
Of whom I'm a part?
Who sent me here,
in the world of more cries than laughs?
What's my goal?
Will I ever be able to rise and spark?
Who loves me?
Who is there in my heart?
Who is there for my sake?
Or are there people only with double face?
Who is going to rest this chaos?
for I resolve this year to put an end to dark.
And suddenly with a ping on screen,
i realized yet another year has passed,
these questions are still a part,
not just mine but of every human heart.

Enwreathed with bounties,
finest persons to dear,
we all think we are living a life of rare.
Taking for granted, all is real,
we believe our pals won't sneer, but
cheer, at every step, at every fear.
Perhaps over expecting only to bear,
to make life more severe, to bring self to tear.
Forgetting, ephemeral is only real,
pals will sneer no matter how dear.
Bounties will come and go,
positivity alone will make you grow.
Remember only givers in life giggle,
expectations make happiness to wriggle.
Your life is your gear,
you alone can make it cheer.

Dear life,

I know you have many lessons to teach,
before it's my time to leave.
Yesterday's brought little sorrow,
gave me pain, made me hollow.
Today's brought all cheers,
to help me forget yesterday's tears.
I am ready to take what's there for tomorrow,
be it cheers or little sorrow,
in the end I know they are all to save me,
from being a moron.

Life does move on,
but forgets to take its memories along,
for they don't make you recollect your happy past,
rather brings a sore realization, nothing forever lasts.

Why life is the way it is?

Why smile comes only after abundance of pain?

Why misery is more lasting than happiness of rain?

Why rays fail to show when it's deadly darker?

Why it has to break a person before it gets to sparkle?

Why its journey is chaotic than filled with bliss of chuckles?

Have feelings,
love, anger, hatred, joy,
don't harbor them.
Have emotions,
but be emotionless.
Unlearn, you learnt,
to learn the best.
The sky belongs to the wings,
not to the burdened nest.

The Life

Life is a gift of God,
don't make it rot.
Live it's elixir to brim,
before it begins to flicker and
become grim.
Shun the thought of cutting its string,
for your life is full of love and
care your pals bring.
Think of all the bounties you have,
till the happiness finally ring.
But don't cut its string,
for a life is a gift,
sing until you become its king.

In the journey of life,
every person you encounter is a mere guest,
some come to garnish your journey with sweet affairs,
some to inflict pain and hurt,
to give you lessons imperative for you to be a sage,
some come to try and impair your flight,
some only to make you fly and rise,
some of them will stay for a while,
some will severe the connection,
in the blink of an eye.
None is going to be there, till the end of your life,
only you and your creator,
have the perennial union, till the time dies.
Bestow your faith and heart in him,
guests may arrive and depart,
but in these encounters,
don't lower your zest and spark.

Oh life! how uncertain you are,
silently you extinguish your spark,
not even once you announce the arrival of dark.
Along with spark, you take away man's very chance,
to top off the work he left in half,
the plans he aspired to give a start,
to enjoy the wealth,
he accumulated for later happy laughs.
You leave behind alone, the suffering pals,
with deep emptiness scars.

Life,
a puppet show,
Almighty its puppeteer,
human his puppet,
acting on his command,
to please his charm.
Not all are able to please,
Almighty has a rule,
one who obey, please,
discover and get release.
Defiance has a different fate,
murkiness is its abode and gate,
salvation is late.
If you aspire to be the spark of his charm
escape the dark, embrace the warm,
love the rich and poor alike,
do no harm and hype.

THE PAIN

Enjoy life it's one, they said,
but gave whole lot to dread.
Don't care, be yourself they said,
selfish the next moment was yelled.
Speak your heart, be true they said,
accusations were all then levied.
Live your dreams, be passionate they said,
responsibilities what they meant.
You are strong, be positive they said,
negativity was the only thing sent.
It's your life they said, and
expectations is all what they held.

Numerous friends and relations I have,
real virtual all so fab,
filled with love care and merriness,
all for moment of happiness.
No one to feel my sad,
to wipe the tears of cry I had,
to listen the inner tune
that make me stifle and mad,
to dispel the hurt and bring the soothe back,
to give me shoulder and relieve me
in the moment of bad.
All there is, is me and my stabs,
manifesting, I alone have the healing power,
to turn them into beautiful scars,
by befriending the only mighty stars.

The Pain

Sometimes somewhere,
despite the people around,
loneness we found.
Despite the love sent,
unloved we felt.
Despite the music in air,
noise was heard in air.
Despite the calm,
mind was constantly alarmed.
Despite the heals and care,
we felt wounded and dared.
Despite the blessings in life,
sometimes somewhere,
curses and death were only in sight.

How I wish,
my next hour,
to be death hour,
for the pals I loved,
turned sour.
The dreams I had,
gives me no power.
Future is filled,
with scenes of horror.
I know I am talking,
like a moron.
O' Almighty!
Please show me,
some ray of light,
take away all these sorrows.
I promise,
I'll prove to be worth living,
thousands of morrows.

The future,
I don't know what it is,
but it looks dark, like a black hole.

I don't know where I am leading,
I am devoid of all hope, all actions,
for I feel like doing nothing,
but to sit and let the day unfold.

All dreams and ambitions are failing,
to inspire me to the point of work,
or perhaps it's my lack of determination
that makes me ignore the once cherished goals.

All relations, attachments and friends,
I feel are failing the test of times and leaving my side,
or perhaps it's my self- hatred and blurry vision,
that makes me doubt,
the loyalty of one's who claim to be mine.

I don't know what it is, where I am leading,
towards prosperity and freedom or self- destruction.

I wish, in the journey,
I encounter a light, a light to tend my chaotic soul,
for I don't want a future,
with meaningless life and rueful soul.

I was winning,
i was full,
it was all shiny,
everything was perfect,
until he asked,
are you alright?

Voice here, voice there,
suffocating me,
in the name of care.
Killing the spirit,
I raise to cheer.
Ignoring the star,
I wish to appear.
Safety being their concern,
my freedom is what they burn.
Thinking it to be great,
my choice is what they break.
Expecting me to be a sage,
even in the gloomy cage.
Supporting is what they say,
with their nose in my way.
Enslaving me to crave,
for the life I wish to brave.

The Pain

It wasn't lone deep stab,
but brutal sharp little pokes,
by the world,
that seeped trust,
from hitherto protected heart.

THE HOPE

Dear self,

Why you look at the uncoloured part?

When your life is full of colourful art.

Why you think of unblessed curses?

When you have blessings in abundance in your purses.

Why you feel the loneliness?

When your own company is holiness.

Why you stick to things that make you wry and cry?

When you have ability to move on and fly.

Why you give birth to frustration and loathing?

When your natural essence is of soothing.

Dear self,

Why you are slumbering in dark?

When you have power to live in spark.

Why you don't shift your sight?

When you can see the real light of life.

Pain never comes alone,
brings a chance to explore,
your own self utterly ignored,
the hidden treasures of your soul,
you never had inkling before,
put an end to feeling its sour,
it has much more for you to explore,
for it is not a penalty for wrong,
but a call for you to grow and be strong.

Don’t listen to the voices,
that says ‘you can’t’.
Have faith in yourself,
you can achieve what you want.
Just give your dreams,
the fuel of efforts it demands.
Certainly one fine day,
you will rise to be one of the shinning stars.

Dear self, I know,

the transition from merry go lucky illusions

of the world you once held,

to the realm of dismal reality that actually dwell,

is making you experience the hell,

to question the very norms of existence

of women and men,

which have nothing but an illusory spell.

But don't be frail, endure the process,

for sailing through it will mark your journey,

from a mere gravel to a precious gem.

Hold on,
not to your pain,
not to your guilt,
it will give you no gain,
but make you wilt.

Hold onto hope,
hope of season of spring,
hope of some missing spice and mint.

If magic is happening of events,
when there is no hope.
If magic is sudden emergence of light,
when all in sight is just black holes.
If magic is getting world's share of pie,
when you believed you deserved a single loaf.
Then yes there exists magic,
the universe surrounding us is magic,
our very existence is magic,
our being where we are is magic,
perhaps we deserved not even a loaf,
our getting a pie is nothing but a magic.

Swirl,
swirl with your frock,
round and round,
with celerity when mind is clouded,
murkiness is wrenching the heart.

Swirl,
to shed away the pain,
the expectations, the failures,
that are captivating the mind and heart.

Swirl,
till the baggage is off,
till the mist is gone,
till the gloom embraces the spark.

Swirl,
till your mind is in rhythm,
with the tune of your heart,
till it feels the treasures and pleasure
in life's unstoppable dance.

Swirl,
swirl with your frock,
round and round,
heartily, before you lose your chance.

THE LOVE

The promise to be together forever,
is lost somewhere in this capricious weather.

Faded away is the love we cherished,
same as the care is perished.

Its terrible feeling when I see you twirling,
in your own world of joy and hue,
unmindful that I may still be in need of you.

I knew, I will become a forgotten cloud,
unaware I was, it will bring pain in my heart,
tears in my eyes too.

I wish sometimes, to halt the time,
to go back to embrace the same shine,
only to realize it's not a dream but a life.

Fake is not my love for you,
I know you might miss me to boot,
people come and go, so as you.

Your presence make me bright,
no matter how hollow you are from inside.
Your every giggle gives me delight,
even when you have learnt to fake smile.
Your every gossip gives me light,
even when your own life has dark insights.
Your promise to be my side,
even when world is trying to slide,
makes my love for you infinite.
Your comforting style,
even when people consider you fright,
awakes the crazy in me to flight.
Dear Friend,
you make me feel alive,
by nourishing the tie we made for life.

From unshed tears to cheer in eyes,
from reel to real in smile,
from weakness to confidence in heart,
from screams to dreams in mind,
from rough to tough in style,
is her journey from love to self- love in life.

Once upon a time,
in a bright sunshine,
she lost her heart to a fancy man.
Who avowed to love it like a mad,
only to be returned with a stab,
chasmic enough, to shun its glam,
to extract all the love and trust she had.
For it was a folly of her brain,
human love is not an antonym of pain,
but it's another name,
in it feelings are not eternal,
but an ephemeral game,
it's the desire that keeps up the flame,
lies and hurt but, are its real name,
broken trust, wounded heart the only gain.

How foolish is the human heart,
for every time love jabs,
it agrees to let the wisdom fall,
to forget the suffering, the pain, the howl,
to embrace its charm merrily,
as a soothing rain in the woe.
Despite the inkling,
it might end like a burning snow.

Sometimes I wonder, how people move on?
How persons who once ruled their heart,
becomes nothing but a faded past?
How unions, once gave a pleasure like first rain,
becomes nothing but a grim substance of pain?
How vows to go till last are dumped merrily,
naming it the need of hour?
I wonder how people move on?
Perhaps, this is how life goes on.

Someday may be someday,
when the sun is bright, sky is clear,
mind is free from all the fear,
soul is strong enough to endure and bear,
I would like to know,
was it so easy to be blind,
to the pain inflicted on my soul,
to pretend all is shine and nothing went sour,
to let slip the memories hitherto,
were the reason of sheer and joy,
to move to the next row with new pals and vows.
Someday, certainly someday,
I would like to know,
was it so easy for him to let everything go,
when we could still have made a castle
as white as snow.

The Love

Love, a feeling,
so right, yet so wrong,
so bright, yet bring with it the dark,
the dark so gloomy that shatters its charm
breaks a person to the point,
from which there is no recovery from the harm.

A perfect love can indeed be a perfect lie,
for the world loves a person
for its achievements and highs,
a failure is always a matter of dislike.
If you are loved be wise,
don't take in it pride,
perhaps it's your rise,
making people to abide,
sans which there is no love and like.

Believe in love,
a love that empowers you,
to hold onto hope,
to hold onto courage,
to hold onto strength,
a strength, you need
to accept the reality of life,
to forgive, the misery of circumstances,
a love, that despite the distance,
despite the age,
flourishes like a fine wine,
not in a love that goads illusion
and is mere butterflies and shine.

In the mist of lust, I thought I lost her trust.
Her ignorance, my resentment gave it bust.
As destined, I lost the link, in just a blink.
New bonds took the lead,
i started feeding them to the need.
Barely realizing, love never ends,
friendship never dies.
Fairly the doubt was short lived,
I got the grip, I lost to fit.
Love was not dead, it was only suppressed.
Care was not gone, it was just not shown.
Today, love is flourished, care is returned,
so as our bond is reborn.

You think I no more love you,
ignoring the prays I make for you.
Yes, for me you have no time,
aloofness, but will not make me blind.
I know you have to shine,
hard work will make you grind.
No more I'm a person,
who ask for your presence and sight.
I know you are always mine,
no matter how busy and far you are from this senile.
Love I know, has a rhyme,
no matter, it is always by your side.

Love not same for all,
but a matter of prior.
Glee, pain and sour,
depends all on your score.
Mindless of the place you give,
to their grace,
comfort is what they chase.
Giving you enough to brave,
for their love, for their sake.

With smiles started a game,
creating a mirage of delight,
love was termed as its plight.
Flowers, chocolates made it bright,
players named it a light.
A light that will make them brave,
to reach all the things they crave.
Soon with the rise,
of expectations and frights,
the light became a gloomy sight,
maring all its early delight,
revealing its true plight,
of just being pomp and show,
not the true love players saw.
For the love face no conditions and freights,
but only the eternal vibes.

THE ALMIGHTY

O dear almighty! shed some light,
how can I not be cynical about people?
how can I keep my heart pure,
and give blessings to all?
When everyday surfaces,
an unacceptable shade
of their blemished soul.

Dear child,
a soul is never blemished,
it's pure and your forever guiding angel,
it's the greed of human's famished mind,
for ephemeral shines,
that subdue the pure angel
and compel them to be a constant changer,
its right to be cynical,
to avoid heart break and danger,
but don't malign your purity,
surpass the layers of shades,
love me and have faith,
for I am there in all, not ephemeral but eternal.

Don't appease the one,

who looks for an illusionary glamour,

bound to wane, in you.

Please the one,

for whom matters the beauty of soul inside you.

The one, certainly is not human,

but the creator, who created this universe and you.

His light gives body a life and grace,
short of which we are mere
fire, dust, water, air and space,
yet people seek pleasure only in shape,
they struggle in their journey for solace,
yet love mere fire, dust, water, air and space
devoiding the soul for the love it crave,
forgetting it is the real grace,
solace lies in loving it not mere
fire, dust water, air and space.

THE SOUL

Oh human!
I was born free, full of glee,
to be a partner in your life spree.
I was the light of love sent your way,
who knew no bar,
to give you courage to fight the dark,
a desire to spark.
I came here to bring you back,
to the mighty star,
of whom I'm a part.

See what you did to my plight,
you took away all my light,
exchanged my love for hatred,
sent only darkness in my sight,
you sold my courage,
for the limitations this world threw upon you.
You chose the bounties of world,
disregarding the faith,
I and my almighty bestowed upon you.
I arranged for you a flight to sky,
but you decided not to fly.
Keeping me down,
along with you for all the cry.

Oh human!
I'm your key to almighty,
abode in heaven is my home
you alone can take me along.

Oh human!
Look at my plight,
please make it delight,
give me back all that is mine.

How can I dream,
of future, fortune,
success and good rapport?
How can I promise,
to world love care and support?
When my every another breathe,
is prisoner of the mighty lord.

Don't stop at the periphery,
thrive to go deep,
it's the dust that float on surface,
real beauty lies deep inside,
in the inner soul,
just like pearls lie deep inside the ocean
to be explored.

My madness has surpassed the brim,
for in the world of ephemerals,
I'm searching for an eternal bliss.

Dear universe,
don't let me fall for the dust again,
I know it's all illusion and vain,
it carries along nothing
but the insurmountable pain,
still it's allure is making
the wisdom misty and insane,
please save me from the drudgery,
I no more have strength,
to let myself into drain,
all I want to feel is your eternal love,
which keeps me happy and sane.

The Soul

I am not my mind,
mind is what it perceives,
senses perceive only the visible,
detach from the mind.

I am not my body,
body is cluster of skin and organs,
made up of air, water, fire, space and soil,
the elements found in every morsel,
detach from the body.

The people I meet are not real,
they are the same cluster,
bound to wear and tear,
detach from people.

I am not my work,
doer of which is the creator of universe,
detach from the work.

If I am, I am the soul,
attaching to the supreme is her only goal.

THE HUMANS

People are not worthy of thy trust,
for a moment thou may think,
thee have one, thou can tittle tattle with,
rely upon when things are worst,
but the other moment,
certainly its going to burst,
leaving thou forlorn with disgust,
better to be precautious from first,
not people, put thy faith in,
thy maker, thyself and thy gut,
for a world is not a place to trust.

I have seen people,
often bowing to the rising sun,
leaving behind the stars,
hitherto were with them in their life's run,
uplifting, healing and having all the fun,
only for some gains and rays of the rising sun.

Dear self,
No matter what you do or don't.
No matter whether you agree
to what people say or not.
They will always scrutinize you.
They will always raise the bars
of rationality and morality to influence you.
They will always pass judgements,
to suppress you.
But don't get swayed away,
these are mere judgements
and bars to break you,
not the real self that makes you, you.

Humans are stories,
stories made up of desires,
disappointments, delicate connections.
Connections, a vital thread to weave a story,
a story that is powerful,
full of love, deceit, affairs of sorry.
People are connections,
connections which materialize,
throughout a story, for a story,
connections some of which are sweet,
bitter sweet,
some bitter with no sweet to a story.
Connections some of which pop up, stay,
travel till the end of story,
some cameo,
some drift apart before it's the end of a story,
connections some of which are snapped,
excluded by a story,
to preserve its glory,
a glory, that transcends a story,
some leave by choice,
some by wait, a wait for being a priority,

a priority that never gets voice,
a voice which emerges as a noise,
beyond the end of story,
a noise which is rueful but futile,
futile because it already ended,
ended, a story, a human,
a human story.

The sun, the moon,
the air, the water,
the green on the earth,
the stars in the sky,
the only constants,
I had and have in
the fall and the cry,
the joy cycle,
that repeats a while,
the struggle, the uproar, the silence
in the progression and the flight.

The humans?
Oh! they have their own plight,
things they have prioritized,
for absence they offer real life excuses,
for their own sake, their own smile.

The sun, the moon,
the air, the water,
the green on the earth,
the stars in the sky,
the [illegible] constitutes,
I [illegible] have in [illegible]
the [illegible] and the [illegible]
the joy cycle
the [illegible]
the thoughts, the emotions, the silence
In the progression and the flight.

The humans
Oh they have their own plight,
things they have prioritized,
for whether they often seal the [illegible],
for their own sakes, their own sake.

For your smile,
he toils million times.
To make you shine,
he burns day and night.
Without a complaint,
he gives you every delight,
ignores himself to make you bright.
Supports you despite all the frights.
Indeed, father is the one,
who loves you infinite.
Glance at your sight,
he is an angel in guise.
For his every effort, pay him right,
earn the star he wish to sight, and
burn so hard to be his pride.

THE HUMANITY

O dear human!

Your greed has made you a moron,

you may grease your palms,

fill your coffers,

kill for fame,

fight for power tomorrow.

Today, have humility,

extend a helping hand,

for your own fellowmen are in sorrow.

The whole world has slipped into penury,
for no one can now afford,
to make people smile,
to check upon their health,
to sit and converse over fine dine,
to spend some quality time,
to extend some healing and shine.
All they can afford,
is cheap gossip, hurt, hatred, deceit and jibe.

Oh human!
you were sent here
to spread love,
you are sowing hatred.

You were sent here
to find the truth,
you are running behind useless pleasures.

You were sent here
to perpetuate trust and peace,
you are burning down things in chaos
for your greed.

You were sent here
to be happy and unfurl glee,
you are being cruel and mean.

You were given reason and logic,
you but are interested only,
in manifesting your animal genes.

Let's speak of love,
for there is no dearth
of hate in the world.

Let's extend a hand
to wipe out some tears,
to let the broken souls know
they are not alone to bear,
for there is no dearth of hands,
full of weapons.

Let's be of some hope,
to let the fallen see their heights again,
for there is no dearth of people,
dragging the masses into dingy drains.

Let's be honest and
make chains of truths,
for the lies and betrayals,
are taking roots.

Let's speak today of love,
to let hate see no triumph.

THE AIM

The Aim

To dive deep,
to surpass all the illusion and myth,
to reach the truth,
to feel the charm and bliss,
is all in my life I wish.

The Aim

It's good to be someone's favourite,
to have company, to have support.
But I want to be,
my own companion, I can enjoy with a lot,
my own support, I can rely upon,
my own favourite, I can be proud of.

THE NATURE

Million pearls pouring on the earth,
resonating to make count its worth.
Dazzling in its shine,
setting every heart on rhyme.
Rejuvenating the very plight,
to bring every delight.
Few fail to feel its bright side,
to have its positive sight,
they keep swirling with their might,
thinking it to be a day without spice,
they shun the soothe rain brings to their life.

He brought me to His kingdom,
gave me life,
to make my plight a delight.
Made trees, mountains, rivers and
other beautiful sights,
to soothe my eyes,
fresh breeze to cool my hype.
Created birds, pigeons, nightingale
for a music to hear,
human beings for a company to cheer,
together to bear sorrows we fear.
Made all arrangements for my feed,
fruits, vegetables all so sweet,
left nothing to dread,
assigned only a task to enrich the life,
with his name to be freed.

I tried to be mightier than Him,
decided to be king of The King,
begin wiping the idyll.
He made trees, I created mansions,
at the cost of their life

and million breathes.
He made breeze to keep my hype,
I made breeze a hype
by adding toxins of all type.
He made birds, nightingale,
for music to hear,
I made cars, planes, horns,
a noise to bear.
He gave me company to cheer,
I made money my dear,
making my existence for a man to fear.
He made feed for my need,
fruits, vegetables all so sweet,
I adulterated them,
to have bumper feed,
for the sake of greed,
for taste made poor animals my seed.
He left nothing to dread,
I made everything a dread,
forgetting my work is to be freed,
His name is my seed.

All I created is not my win,
but a sin I committed to the brim.
Despite his warn signs,
floods, tsunami and slides,
I kept close my eyes,
remained busy giving frights.
Perhaps near is the time
to pay my price,
to face the King and His might,
for all the damage,
I did to His sight.

O rain!
who you are?
A noise or a song,
a season or a storm,
a burn or a balm,
a chaos or a calm,
or you have,
both paradoxical charms?

Certainly you are powerful,
to act as a balm on painful scars,
to bring in soothe and calm,
to rejuvenate a season,
of flourish and flower,
to reverberate a song,
rekindling a desire in heart,
to fly and dance,
to rise to the glow and spark.

Yet you bring in the noise of past,
the burns of memories,
long ago termed as dark,

the chaotic battle of right and wrong,
giving rise to unsettling storm
between a mind and heart,
which was thought,
to be finally gone and left in the past.

THE NATION

Years of independence,
are we really free?

Where religion is the king of mind,
humanity is just a sign.
Where killing is just,
in the name of divine,
helping is dust on its shine.
Where custom still takes the lead,
right is on the back seat.
Where footpaths are for sleep,
junk piles for million's meal.
Where women are still,
treated as machines,
for the pleasure deals.
Where society blames the right,
save the crime.
Where children are unsafe,
youth is in drain,
and corruption is the game.
Can that nation be called unchained?

To make your nation truly free,
take a plea,
make humanity your seed,
give right the lead,
religion the back seat,
be a human, not just the other breed.
Respect the women, save the child,
blame the crime, not the right.

The rulers may dream,
they are king today.
They must not go far in dreaming,
for their kingdom is nothing,
but a dingy jail.

Where eatables are no more,
an essential sale,
everything else is on sale.
Where economy is frail,
focus is only on election parades.
Where temples of God,
and democracy are on rise,
displaying humanity
and democratic values is proscribed.

Where their tongues need,
the taste of lavish foods in forts,
the farmers are on roads,
fighting for rights on their own fields,
which rulers tried to suppress
by playing a cheat.

Where criminal is awarded
a position of lawmaker,
the giver of food is brandished
as trouble maker.

Where there is train of blind disciples
at their command,
with no brains and art,
who see no blood, tears or pains,
only the favours
they grease their palms with
and some other dirty gains,
TRP, monopoly or a heated fame.

Where women are unsafe,
common man is still struggling
for its rights,
facing the inflated prices,
braving the heat and cold together,
the rulers are busy filling their coffers.

Yes, the rulers may dream
they are king today,
they must wake up
before comes the doomsday,
the time to face the real king,
to answer for all the sins.

With heavy but hollow eloquence,
with web stories and short remembrance,
your so called elite children,
celebrated your independence.
Independence,
which they claimed to be gained,
with blood shed and arrows of gloom,
by freeing you from shackles of foreign rule,
to make you in your own land,
breathe and soothe.

Is this really your independence mother India,
or a license to your elite children,
to suffocate your breathe further and rule,
to suppress and bleed your children,
to make you swoon,
children who have no voice of their own,
for whom your independence,
has no significance,
for their plight is still the same dinginess.
Indeed it's an illusory freedom
making your heart bleed,

seeing your own children fight and steal,
shackling you harder only to make you reel.
I wish, your children open their eyes,
see their mother still cries,
for the love, for the brotherhood,
for the freedom,
they all owe her since their rise,
before it's too late to be wise.

With dreams in the eyes,
spirits so high, leaving their land,
my pals entered your sky.
Fancing every bait,
you offered to chase, will make their fate,
unaware of the hurdles,
you have on your gate.
From high fees to unheard pleas,
snatched all their glees.
From jobs to the mobs,
suppressed were their silent sobs.
From domestic chores, to need for study,
made their life to scurry.
Stress for real really made them bear,
homesickness aggravated their fear,
leaving their high spirits in tear.
In such time all they need is some cheer,
I hope my pals get a hand,
that undo their fear,
give them feel they are dear.
And the foreign land is like their own
neither to cry, nor to shy,
but indeed to fly.

A WOMAN

A Woman

Shackled by customs,
trapped in traditions,
why a woman is always made
to suppress her ambitions?
She too has her goals,
she too has her wishes,
why her liberty is put at stake
due to your unknown fears?
World is not bad,
it's your illusion that puts you back.
At least once see it through her tears,
it's hard to live like,
a bird without feathers.
Look at her plight,
she wants to make it delight.
Just give her chance,
to prove her stance.

A Woman

Seeker of love was she,
always making her pleas,
to the shine, to the fine,
to the free.
Unheard went all her appeals,
lowing her spirit,
making her silly,
such silly,
when love knocked on her door,
she bolted it calling it a joke.

Clouds are giving music,
to the whirlpool in her heart,
groaning ferociously,
shooting questions,
hitherto she refused to dart.

You think you are a king,
I'm your slave.
You assume,
you have a right to do the sin,
to settle you sexual crave.
You outraged my modesty,
stabbed my freedom,
gave me pain, and
a social stain,
leaving enough for me to brave.
This but, does not make me afraid,
I'm a fighter, not a slave,
will regain all that is drained.
You indeed not a king, but a frail,
who consider it pleasure,
to bring the shame,
upon the one who created your name.

She had all chance to fame,
a gleaming fire to reign,
an ability for the same,
she chose to give me name.
Disregarding the glare,
impairing her frame,
she gave me life,
bearing all the pain.
After toiling for the day,
leaving her solace,
she spent sleepless nights,
embracing me for my sake.
Dumping her dreams,
ignoring all the blames,
she is a supporter in all my games.
After all her lost battles,
the biggest gain is her family, she thinks.
Despite all the hurt,
comfort is all she gives,
happiness is what she brings.
She is a mother,
a queen indeed, without whom
your existence is what you can't think.

Yes it looks wrong,
not that its wrong,
but because a girl is doing it.
Threatening the privileges,
hitherto granted to you alone.
Challenging the dominance,
you practiced infinitely all over the world.
Devoiding you of superiority,
you thought is exclusively your zone.

For how long?
the world is going to reject me for,
the colour of my skin,
the amount of fat collected within,
the short frame of physique I got,
for which I have no choice but to fit in,
the lack of protruded curves,
that makes me less feminine,
the abundance of locks,
all around the frame,
I chose not to trim.

May be sometime, somewhere,
it will embrace what is inbuilt,
and let go of rejection,
to accept me with a grin,
for it hurts to be punished,
for an uncommitted sin.

Take me back to those days,
when I could dress up freely.
Sans the fear of checking,
ever strip and seam is on place.
Sans the fear of becoming,
object of judgement and shame.
Sans the trouble,
of plucking the peeping locks
and enduring the pain.
Sans the lustful eyes,
striping me nake.
Sans the fear of falling their prey.
Take me back,
for I wish to swirl in my frill frock
and laugh heartily once again.

Oh you! magnificent creator,

You created birds,
made sky their limit,
which itself has no limit.

You created copious sea creatures,
made depth of oceans their abode,
which itself is immeasurable.

You created peculiar land animals,
made forests, roads, streets,
for their safe heaven,
which itself guarantee their,
unrestrained roam and travel.

You created men,
gave them unbridled position,
which itself ensured,
their indomitable power.

Then you created women,
but why you forgot to give them,
unlimited favour?
Why you confined their life,
to the wills and fancies,
of their neighbors?
Why you left them,
with no option but to savour?

Dear mothers,

your children are adorable,

they are cunning and selfish too.

It's an illusive trap of love and care,

they lay around you to bound you.

Don't be swayed away,

too much in their emotions.

For when they leave

it will be tough for you to hold up.

Indeed it's you responsibility to look after,

but don't be ignorant to your own right

of some peace and laughter.

A Woman

She may look sugar and sweet,
be observant and careful,
before you mess with her.
She wears an invisible crown,
the charm of which
you won't be able to bear.
She holds an invisible sword,
the sight of which you must always fear.
For she is not a girl with makeup,
any longer, you can easily peer.
She is, but a girl with indomitable,
confident demeanor,
of which you must be aware.

THE ILLUSION

An illusion,
a dream, we all are living in,
a false reality,
we all wish to keep swaying in,
a despicable charm,
cast upon our vision to keep it blur,
a futile journey of hurt and happiness,
we take for comfort.

How I wish illusion,
to be not an illusion,
rather a truth, I thought it to be,
a fantasy, I wanted to live in,
a comfort pill, once I wanted to take in,
it was, but a charm, meant to break in.

Having the taste of the truth,
it is hard to be mocked by illusion again,
but how I wish,
living in truth to be as undemanding,
as living in illusion was,
to be as solacing as illusion was.

It is wise to be ripe from raw,
even amidst the ripeness,
how I still wish it to be the truth,
not the blown out dream I once saw.

We all have dreams to dear,
passion to cheer,
which reflects our souls,
depicting the principles we bear,
things that make us real.
We, but live in fear,
to reveal the personality we revere,
to the society,
which claims to be superior.
Dreading its branding our ideals,
to be inferior,
we begin to conceal them,
considering it to be convenient.
Forgetting, pleasure lies in real living,
not in the illusions we are giving.

THE SUCCESS

Aiming to be stars,
busy frittering hours,
living in fantasy,
forgetting that time has a bar,
is this how you aim to spark?

Time is an evermoving flow,
letting it go as a cost of happiness,
will surely secure a place for you in murkiness.
Twenty-four hour in a day is all you have,
to be the star you aspire and crave.
Hard work is a cue, focus is an answer,
hold it before it holds you.
Time is a flow, follow its row,
Letting it go,
will later make you regret and low.

Adding to he stars

Busy fretting hours

living in fantasy

forgetting that you [illegible]

is that how you aim to speak

[illegible] overcoming Time

[illegible]

[illegible]

[illegible]

to the [illegible] you aspire and crave.

[illegible]

[illegible]

[illegible]

Letting it go,

with little chance to regain [illegible]

Shunning its harm to the core,
comfort is all we lure,
thinking it to be the cure,
to the agonies, to the sour.
Building a shell around, to be secure,
we close the door for the more.
Letting opportunities to fall on the floor,
on the name of it being futile and bore,
vainly hoping life to pour,
all its blessings on our store.
Life will, pour it on your store,
first break the shell, which made you sour,
then collect the score, you left on floor, and
roar it is not bore, but a door to the zion.

THE ESCAPE

When tongue fails,

pen trails.

Are people worthy of thy trust,
friendship, loyalty, time,
or all the emotional healing
thee give to uplift and bring them a smile?
when all thee are going to have at the end,
is thy pen and thy rhyme.

The Escape

When my heart is at war,
when my mind is filled,
with gloom and sour,
poetry is an escape,
where lies my solace and soul.

9 789363 307018

Printed by Libri Plureos GmbH in Hamburg,
Germany